What Is Your Issue?

Shaun Andrews

ISBN 979-8-89428-146-9 (paperback)
ISBN 979-8-89526-189-7 (hardcover)
ISBN 979-8-89428-147-6 (digital)

Christian Faith Publishing
832 Park Avenue
Meadville, PA 16335
www.christianfaithpublishing.com

Printed in the United States of America

*To my Lord and Savior, Jesus Christ, for giving
me the privilege of writing this book.*

*To my late father, Deacon Isaac D Andrews, and my
mother, Hazel B Andrews, who, by the leading of the
Lord, made me the servant and leader I am today
For that, I am forever grateful, and I honor them.*

Contents

Introduction

In this book, I want to talk about issues. We all have them, and we must meet them head-on with the help of the Holy Spirit. God has placed inside us everything we need to cope during our issues or to be completely healed. If we are not healed from the issue on this side of life, God will enable us to live with it. You can live with the issue through the aid of the Holy Spirit; it does not have to overtake you. Apostle Paul in the Bible had a thorn in his flesh (2 Corinthians 12:7).

This book's *purpose* is to help us recognize our issues and apply the scriptures from the Word of God so it can be a tool to help us. My testimony will be an example of God's healing power and mercy.

Salvation

The first step we need to take to be healed from our issue is to be born again. Romans 10:9–10 lets us know that if we confess with our mouth the Lord Jesus and believe in our heart that God has raised Him from the dead, we shall be saved, "for with the heart, man believes unto righteousness; and with the mouth, confession is made unto salvation." That is the first step on your way to overcoming an issue.

What is your issue?

Personal Inventory Questions

1. What is your issue or issues?

2. What is the devil trying to use in your life to cause you not to walk in victory?

3. What testimony are you working on?

4. What has the devil thrown your way to stop your progress?

What Is Your Issue?

We all have an issue or maybe even many issues on this side of life. What is the devil trying to use in your life to cause you not to walk in victory? Or, what is God allowing in your life so He can work it out for your good?

Romans 8:28 (NLT) says, "And we know that God causes everything to work together for the good of those who love God and are called according to His purpose for them."

What testimony are you working on? Get it in your mind right now! What has the devil thrown your way to stop your progress? What is your issue?

In Luke 8:22–25, Jesus and His disciples were on a boat, and as they sailed, Jesus took a nap. But soon a very bad storm came down the lake. The boat was filling with water. They were in real danger. The disciples went and woke Jesus up, shouting, "Master, Master, we're going to drown!"

Faith

Jesus woke up and rebuked the wind and raging waves. The storm stopped, and all was calm. Then Jesus asked them, "Where is your faith?"

Is your issue a lack of faith? Is there a storm in your life?

You know, often winds start blowing in our personal lives. It may be a loss of a loved one. It may be a sickness that hits our body. We could have a financial crisis. Whatever it is, the winds of trouble may try to shake our faith. Sometimes, if it is not one thing, it is something else.

Troubling Winds

Have you gone through something that felt like a hurricane or a tsunami, an attack after attack from the enemy? Sometimes they knock us down to our knees. Sometimes the wind blows us down right on our faces. Yes, the winds are going to blow, but we need a foundation in God. Because I found out that when the troubling winds blow and knock us down, that is the best place to be. It is hard to stumble when we are on our knees, and God will be there to give us peace. One word from the Lord will calm the storm in our lives.

Have you ever been through a situation that felt like a hurricane or a tsunami in your life? If so, what was it?

Touch His Hem

We must touch the hem of Jesus's garment, so to speak, like the woman with the issue of blood. You know, when we look at her story in the Bible, she had been to many doctors over the twelve years, and she was no better. And she grew worse. You see, our issues can only be healed by Jesus. Even if man could, they are limited, but Jesus has all power. The woman with the issue of blood was going to the doctors, and she was spent.

Testimony

Can I share something with you? Like this woman, I had an issue of blood, and I went to doctors for many years until I, too, touched the hem of Jesus's garment with my faith. That was not my only issue. I struggled for years with my emotions, my physical health, and my financial stability. Like the woman with the issue of blood, I had to push past others' opinions and negative thoughts. I made my way to Jesus for myself, and He took away my sickness, my pain, and my confusion and restored me.

Personal Inventory Questions

1. Is your issue a lack of faith?

2. Are there storms in your life?

3. What do you need the Lord to do?

Testimony

I went to the doctor for years. I was in and out of the hospital. I even had medical issues that my mother succumbed to, but the Lord didn't let me die with those issues! Because I touched Jesus and got desperate, I believed that God was willing and able to restore me. I had to take the steps needed for my healing. Oh yes, there are steps we must take for our healing to manifest.

The first thing I had to do was obey the doctors whenever possible. Then I had to advocate for myself. I had to speak up because my life was at stake. I had to ensure I was taken seriously and treated with respect. I also had to change my eating habits and exercise more. That helped me physically and reduced my stress. I had to pray for wisdom and direction for my health and total life. I had to use my faith and work with God, avoiding anything that would hinder my healing. Most of all, I had to be obedient in every area of my life, and I prayed without ceasing.

To be healed from our issues, we must be obedient and totally surrender to Jesus.

I had to put my spiritual health first and also work on my mental and emotional health at the same time because we are made of three parts: *spirit*, *soul*, and *body*. We all have issues, but we must work with the Holy Spirit to be healed or cope as God ministers in our weakness. I will be the first to tell you that our issue may never completely go away—for example, high blood pressure. However, if we seek the Lord about our issues and do not ignore them, we may never suffer a stroke or a heart attack. Again, the Lord may not take away the issue, but He is able to give us wisdom to be protected with the issue.

What is your issue?

Personal Inventory Questions

1. Will you take the step the Lord gives you for your health?

2. Will you be obedient to the doctors when it is possible?

3. Will you advocate for yourself?

4. Will you make the changes that you know you should?

Back to Life

Around the same time Jesus was dealing with the woman who had the issue of blood, He was interrupted by a leader of the synagogue, Jairus. His daughter had died, and when Jesus heard what happened, He told Jairus, "Don't be afraid. Just have faith, and she will be healed." When Jesus got to her, He took her by the hand and said loudly, "My child, get up!"

At that moment, her life returned to her, and she was able to stand. Jairus's issue was his daughter had died. *What is your issue?* Are there dead things in your life that need to be resurrected?

Don't Be Afraid

I have had things die in my life that Jesus breathed on and brought back to life. No, I didn't have a dead daughter like Jairus, but I have had someone that I poured my all into—my hopes and my dreams. And one day they were gone. Only Jesus could bring them back to life. Let me share with you that I am not a big-time leader in the synagogue. I may be a lot like you reading this book. You may also have a dead situation you are dealing with. You may have a dilemma that seems impossible. Jairus's daughter was dead; it couldn't have gotten any worse. But Jesus heard what happened and told him, "Don't be afraid." That should remind us that Jesus already knows about all our problems, and after we have prayed to Him, we have to say, "Your will be done" and not be afraid. Jesus has heard about our problem, and He is omniscient; He is all-knowing. We can count on Him.

Once, when Jesus was climbing out of a boat, a man possessed by demons came out to meet Him. For a long time, he had been homeless and naked, living in a cemetery outside the town. As soon as he saw Jesus, he shrieked and fell down in front of Him. Then he screamed, "Why are You interfering with me, Jesus, Son of the Most High God? Please, I beg You, don't torture me!" The man knew Jesus already commanded the evil spirit to come out of him by His power and authority. This spirit had often taken control of the man. Even when he was placed under guard and put in chains and shackles, he simply broke them and rushed out into the wilderness, completely under the demon's power (Mark 5:1–5).

Oppressed, Not Possessed

Now, we as Christians cannot be possessed by the devil, but if we let him, he will oppress us. Remember, all sickness is of the devil, and he will even try to control God's property. Yes, even the anointed of God. We have to recognize when the enemy is at work because he is walking back and forth, seeking whom he may devour (1 Peter 5:8).

What is your issue? Have you had this issue for twelve years, twelve months, twelve days, or twelve hours? Don't just sweep it under the rug. Deal with the issue. Let Jesus deliver you from your issue. He can, and He will; only trust Him.

Personal Inventory Questions

1. How long have you had this issue or issues?

2. Do you believe that God is willing and able to heal your issue(s)?

3. If He doesn't, do you believe He will keep you in the issue(s)?

Manifestation

When I think about 1 Samuel 1, it talks about Hannah. Hannah means favor and grace. So when someone called her name, they were saying she was favored and graced by God.

But Hannah wasn't experiencing the grace and favor the way she wanted to because she had no children at that time. Have you ever been through a season in your life where someone kept speaking blessings over you, and you were waiting for it to manifest?

I remember going to a church out of town years ago, and the pastor would take up an offering for whomever she felt the Lord was leading her to bless.

I said to myself, "One of these Sundays, maybe God is going to use this ministry to bless me."

Well, the pastor is a prophetess, and every time she got near me, she would tell me how prosperous I was and how I was walking in abundance. At that time, what I could see in the natural and put my hands on was pitiful. I didn't have the manifestation yet, and I definitely wasn't seeing in the Spirit. So I can see how Hannah struggled with what her name meant.

Now, if my name meant victory and all I felt was defeat, it would not matter to me until victory came alive in my spirit. It's not enough for someone else to know you're victorious; you need to know it yourself. And I want to tell you, you have the victory. But you have to walk in faith for it to manifest.

Personal Inventory Questions

1. Do you know you will be victorious over your issue?

2. Do you know Jesus died and rose again with all power in His hand to make you free in Him?

3. Do you know you don't have to be weighed down by an issue?

Surrender It

Some of us may have to do like Hannah before it's over, pray, and tell God this and mean it: "Lord, deliver me from this issue and bless me, and I will give it back to You." What do you need to give back to God? If you release it, you can receive it!

Hannah said, "If You give me a child, I'll give him back to You." She sowed him as a seed and reaped a harvest because she had more children. In fact, she had five more children after she gave Samuel back to God.

Don't hold on to your seed if it needs to be offered back to the Lord. When her issue was over, I believe she could say God was the God of more than enough (El Shaddai). He is the all-sufficient one. He is the God that surely answers prayer. After the Lord opened her womb, I believe she would say God is Yahweh Yireh. He will provide.

I believe she knew that He is Yahweh Rapha, the Lord that heals. I believe she would be a witness that He is our banner, Yahweh Nissi. He is Yahweh Raah, our Shepherd.

She Saw Him Differently

I believe she could say the Lord will provide! He is Jehovah Jireh, and when she received what she had been praying for many years and became pregnant, the God of peace restored her peace.

The lack of peace could also be someone's issue. What is your issue?

I believe she saw God in another way when that issue was over.

Have you ever experienced a situation, and when you came out of it, you were in a new place in God? Nothing could shake your faith. You could see Him more clearly. You may have been through the fire, but you came out as pure gold.

When you came out of your situation, you knew for yourself who God was. You had your own experience and testimony. You no longer relied on your mother's relationship with Him, but you knew God had brought deliverance in your life.

So how long will you mourn over what didn't work out in your life? When will you let go of what you lost? When will you move on from what has been taken from you—your past sins, failed relationships, whatever it was? Are you ready to release this issue from your past and have a new beginning? God's ready, but if you're not, He will wait until you get the right attitude of faith. I know it takes a while for us to take that leap of faith and trust the Lord, but He will help us every step of the way.

I am a living example of what God can do!

The three biblical figures I talked about in this book had faith to go to Jesus about their issues. The woman with the issue of blood was told by Jesus, "Your faith has made you well." Jesus told Jairus not to be afraid and to just have faith, and his request from the Lord was granted. Hannah stopped her crying, grabbed onto her faith, and truly received favor and grace. These people got their healing. The demon-filled man was delivered from his issues, and even the girl who died was raised up by Jesus!

Personal Inventory Questions

1. How do you see God now? Has he gotten larger in your eyes?

2. Has your faith been stretched?

3. Has God done the work in your life?

*****

I join my faith with yours right now and say, "Yes, God has!"

Closing Thoughts

Let Jesus be Dr. Jesus in your case.

Even the disciples on the boat, as I mentioned, had an issue or two. Jesus changed their situation. What about you today? Where is your faith?

What is your issue?

Prayer for Issues

Father,

We thank You and we praise You. You are the only wise God, and You don't make mistakes. Father, You have made us in Your image and likeness, and for that, we say thank You. Lord, we thank You for Jesus's sacrifice on Calvary's cross to pay for our sin, as well as heal and deliver us from our issues.

Give us the faith to take our burdens to Your Son and leave them there. Help us deal with what's going on in our lives, minds, health, and finances. Help us remember You sent Jesus so we could be whole in every area. The issue that no one knows about but us and You—God, touch there and bring divine intervention. Stop the pain, hurt, and confusion. Heal our issues. We know You are ready, willing, and able. We know You can do anything but fail. And, Father, if for some reason any of our issues don't leave us totally, You will enable us to see Your strength is made perfect in our weakness. We trust You in the process. We claim victory in Jesus' mighty, powerful, and holy name. Amen.

Father, we thank You for working out our issues and restoring us. No one could do it but You. We say thank you for Your touch on this day.

Scriptures and Bible Verses Used

Scriptures

- 2 Corinthians 12:7
- Romans 8:28
- Luke 8:22–25
- Luke 8:43–48
- Mark 5:1–5
- 1 Peter 5:8
- 1 Samuel 1
- Romans 10:9–10

Bible versions used

- New Living Translation
- King James Version
- English Standard Version
- New King James Version

Acknowledgments

I would like to thank the following people for their encouragement, input, and prayers while I completed this book:

- Ms. Mary L. Andrews
- Rev. Victor and Judi Russell
- Mr. Danny M. Gray
- Mr. Mitchell Ford

About the Author

Shaun S. Andrews is a native of Maple Hill, North Carolina. She grew up and was educated in Onslow County. Shaun was reared in a faith-based home and accepted Jesus Christ as her Lord and Savior in 1994. Shaun has served in the house of the Lord ever since she was a child. She is an ordained minister and the founder of Shaun Andrews Ministries and The Onslow Sisters in the Word Bible Study and Prayer Group. Shaun takes her evangelistic ministries everywhere she goes and believes in the Great Commission. Mark 16:15 says, "He said to them, 'Go into all the world and preach the gospel to all creation.'"

www.ingramcontent.com/pod-product-compliance
Lightning Source LLC
Chambersburg PA
CBHW040117150726
48005CB00013B/1762